GOD IS ALL, IN ALL

GOD
IS ALL
IN ALL

THE EVOLUTION
OF THE CONTEMPLATIVE
CHRISTIAN SPIRITUAL
JOURNEY

HOMEBOUND PUBLICATIONS
BERKSHIRE MOUNTAINS, MASS.

HOMEBOUND PUBLICATIONS

WWW.HOMEBOUNDPUBLICATIONS.COM

© 2012, 2018, 2022 TEXT BY THOMAS KEATING

Cover Design and Interior Design by Leslie M. Browning
Cover Image: © Jay Mantri

First Edition Trade Paperback 978-1-953340-54-2
First Edition Hardcover (Wayfarer Books 2023) 9781956368451
Also Available in eBook, Hardcover and Audiobook

10 9 8 7 6 5 4 3 2 1

Homebound Publications is committed to ecological stewardship.
We greatly value the natural environment and invest in
conservation. For each book purchased in our online store we
plant one tree.

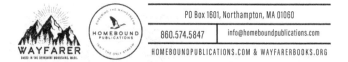

PO Box 1601, Northampton, MA 01060

860.574.5847   info@homeboundpublications.com

HOMEBOUNDPUBLICATIONS.COM & WAYFARERBOOKS.ORG

contents

INTRODUCTION

*A Note from the Contemplative Outreach
by Carl J. Arico, Mary Anne Best & Betty Sue Flowers*

---

*"For Christians, it is to be a kind of fifth Gospel: to become
the word of God and to manifest God empty of self and full of God.*
—THOMAS KEATING, *THE HUMAN CONDITION*

G*od is All in All* is an edited transcript of a keynote talk that Fr. Thomas gave at the 2012 Annual Conference of Contemplative Outreach in Snowmass, Colorado.* From his place of transition at St. Joseph's Abbey in Spencer, Massachusetts in July 2018, Fr. Thomas gave his permission for the editors to edit and publish his talk in book form. We feel very privileged to have done so.

As always, Fr. Thomas challenges and engages us with his teachings and the vastness of their range:

- the infinite compassion and mercy of God
- the three stages of the transformational spiritual journey
- the new cosmology, human nature, science, and their relationship to spirituality
- the message of the cross for our times the meaning of redemption
- and more

The love of God and encouragement shone forth from Fr. Thomas' teaching. He spoke out of his lived experience, and to have been in his presence was to know this and to be enlivened by it. This was a life we wished to know, too! *Go forth, go forth fearlessly with this God of infinite mercy*, he seemed to say.

> *Think of God in a very big way. And if you do, that is too small! You cannot think of anything more wonderful than this God. And you cannot figure out anything about God without a special grace.*

> *God is so marvelously good, there is no word for it. So gentle. So considerate. So kind, so tender—so everything marvelous. That is God. And whatever you say is far less than it is. As Paul says, It hasn't crossed the imagination of any human being what God has prepared for those who love him.*

As a special gift, we have included an "Afterword" with highlights from the homily and eulogy spoken during Fr. Thomas memorial Mass, November 15, 2018. We celebrate the life, legacy, and sending forth of Thomas Keating. May we embody his teachings and bring light to the world.

This work was prepared with prayer and blessing. The editors offer you our prayerful support as you consent ever deeper to the presence and action of God—dying to a limited separate-self sense and becoming deified in Christ. May you be blessed with grace in place of grace as you grow in humility to experience the grandeur of life and welcome it in all its many phases. May you be transformed in Christ for the greater good of all creation. We are not our own; we belong to everyone else.

... for we are members of one another.

EPHESIANS 4:25

FOREWORD

___

by Adam Bucko

There I was, sitting on a Greyhound bus, a 19-year-old moving towards the unknown. I was there because someone convinced me that I needed God in my life and that going to a monastery would help me heal the many traumas of my childhood. These traumas were a consequence of growing up in a totalitarian state in Eastern Europe, against which even my loving family could not offer protection. The journey turned out to be a terrifying ordeal, a kind of initiation into faith. Shortly after leaving New York City, our bus got into a severe accident trapping us inside until rescue workers cut out the door with a chainsaw. We eventually ended up on another bus, only to discover that the driver kept missing his exits, fomenting a kind of mutiny from some of the frustrated passengers. Over ten hours behind schedule, we finally limped into our destination. Little did I know how much healing was awaiting me there.

The monastery to which I felt called was outside the Christian tradition because in those days many of us Christian kids felt that Eastern traditions were the only place to learn real spirituality. I didn't even know that the Church taught meditation and contemplation, so imagine my surprise, when many of the Hindu monks at the monastery spoke to us of the wonders of the Christian mystical tradition. It was in that monastery that I was first drawn to the teachings of Thomas Keating. Every night before bed, my roommate read from *Open Mind, Open Heart,* a recently released book that offered an overview of the history of contemplative prayer in the Christian tradition, and a step-by-step guide on Centering Prayer, the method of contemplative prayer developed by Father Thomas and his fellow Trappist Monks.

Hearing about Centering Prayer was interesting but, at that point in my life, I wasn't persuaded to practice it. Instead, I found my way into another form of contemplative prayer which asked me to connect my breath to a prayer phrase. After a decade or so of this practice, however, it began feeling like something needed to change. The constant activity of repeating a prayer phrase began feeling like I was trying to catch God with constant inner activity. It's seemed like my whole being was longing to "stop doing" and to just "rest in the arms of the Divine." It is then that I re-discovered Father Thomas, and for the first time, saw the brilliance of his teachings on Centering Prayer and receptive silence. Re-discovering his teachings changed everything for me, for within months, I was moved into a receptive way of being, where the gift of God's presence began visiting me in unexpected times and places.

The practice of Centering Prayer was especially helpful in my work with unhoused youth on the streets of New York City, where I was able to understand that I needed to show up for street youth in the same way that I was showing up for prayer. My posture of receptivity allowed me to bear witness to the pain of the world in a new way. My being okay with putting all I knew aside and being in the state of contemplative not-knowing, helped me to not get in the way, so that the Divine could be the one who initiates action. Ultimately it helped me to understand that "prayer and activity are not enemies" and that our actions, especially actions for healing and justice, when done in this contemplative way, can unite contemplation and action and become engaged contemplation.

When I finally came to know Father Thomas in the final decade of his life, our meeting happened in the context of him mentoring the movement that I was co-leading called "new monasticism," a group dedicated to combining monastic spirituality with work for justice. I remember preparing to meet this esteemed spiritual master at his monastery in Colorado. Over the course of three days, we met each day for two-hour long meetings and that was the beginning of my learning from him. Meeting him in person surprised me as he defied my initial expectations. I thought I would meet a brilliant spiritual master who could cut through to the heart and not waste time on frivolities. Instead, meeting him felt like meeting a spiritual grandfather who was very gentle and human, who was interested in the details of my life, someone who cared deeply about justice, and who shared about his own journey with openness and care. Each day we would spend hours talking and sharing. Initially, it felt like we didn't talk about anything significant, but the moment I left our meetings and began walking back to my hermitage I would discover the deep significance of everything Father Thomas and I had discussed. The very energy of our meeting continued to shine light on my life and reveal insights about my vocation and how it needed to be lived.

At other times, especially in our new monastic gatherings, Father Thomas would indeed show up differently. I remember the many occasions he was presented with a question from one of the young new monastics, where he humbly responded that he wasn't sure if he had anything relevant to say on that particular topic, after which we would witness a sort of "download" of spiritual vision that emanated from him. And especially in the last couple of years of his life, sometimes one got a feeling that his joke, "I am trying to forget about myself," had been realized, as there seemed to be very little left of 'him.' What was visible, instead, was a transparent frame though which the Holy Presence could shine.

The book that you are holding in your hands is a true gift. It is the fruit of a life both lived and prayed well. I invite you to read it with an open heart and taste some of the holiness that lived in and taught through Father Thomas. May his witness help you touch something of God in you. May his words infuse you with courage to say "Yes" to becoming God's partner in transfiguring this world.

one

THE SPIRITUAL JOURNEY

The awareness that there is an Other seems to be an invitation to join in the divine life. This is the time for practices that reduce the obstacles enough to be transformed by the divine goodness and Presence.

People have different meanings for God, and there are almost as many words for God as there are people. This isn't a bad insight, because in my understanding, this Being-beyond-being—whoever he, she, or it is—well, there is just no word or concept to embrace it all. It's not so much overwhelming as monumental.

It pervades everything so that this Presence—my favorite word for God—is in everything without being limited to anything. It just is. This is the Mystery that has created us with such great love so that each of us is primarily God or at least participating in God before we are anything else. God is more us than we are, because we were in the mind of God forever, and we will be with God in the fullness of time forever.

Within this context, I hope to give a brief summary of the spiritual journey from the point of view of human nature, of humanity, namely that which even precedes religion. You have to be a little flexible in listening to me.

I see three stages to the spiritual journey by which I understand the transformational process that is at the heart and soul of creation. It seems to me, based on my minuscule experience, that the plan from revelation is that the spiritual journey captures something about human nature and our relationship to this Isness. We should not even say Isness because that is a noun, and God is always active.

God is more like a verb, is-ing all the time and inviting us to is, too. What that involves may take us a lifetime to understand. It is an incomprehensively beautiful vision— only the Ultimate Goodness could have thought it up.

The first step of our spiritual journey, we might say, is the realization—not just a vague acknowledgment, but the realization—that there is an Other (capital O), which goes by many names in Christian and secular history from the beginning. Everyone has developed a cultural name for Issy. It is the awareness that there is an Other, and that we have to do something about this, to accept what seems to be an invitation to join in this life, which is the divine life. And, what's more, this Other seems to be interested in finding out what it is like to be in human life. We begin to feel interested in finding out what it is like to be in God's life and love, too. This is our conversion.

This starts us on a conversion of our life which is a relationship with whatever Is is. Whatever, God knows, is. As soon as one glimpses this, there "It Is" and has always been there. Here we are then at the first step of our spiritual life—the realization that we have to enter into a relationship with the Source of our being that is also reaching out to us in some way that we do not understand, and which manifests in our desire for happiness. Such a desire is perhaps the greatest proof of God's existence. Where else would the desire come from? Certainly not from us earth-bound folks.

The second stage, meaning a perspective on a new life, is to become the Other, and that is the basis of most spiritual literature: how do you become the Other (capital "O")? How do you respond to the invitation that you become the Other? In our Christian perspective, the Other, of course, is Jesus Christ, the Word of God made human in whom God is experiencing what human life is like. God must have wanted to do so because whatever God wants to do, is. This is the time for some discipline. This is the time for practices that enable us to reduce the obstacles or to hang out with God enough to be transformed by the inherent communication of the divine goodness and Presence twenty-four hours a day.

Suppose you become the Other—what happens to Jesus? The friendship of becoming the Other, the invitation of Christ, which has reached some degree of realization, is going to disappear.

Why? Because you have become Jesus, too. In other words, you cannot see your own face. You might if you look in the mirror, but it is not you. When Jesus becomes you, and you become Jesus, you do not see anything. It is a void, you might say, or a sharing in the divine experience of being nothing. Because where did the Word come from—the eternal Word of God or Son of God? He came out of the begetting of the Father who might be called all possibilities. The Son is all possibilities actualized. Hence, "Word" is a good image of what is happening—not that it can contain the reality, because nothing can fully be God except God.

What then could the third step be? There is a third step. Now you have become united with Jesus Christ so much that you cannot distinguish yourself from Jesus in his divine-human nature anymore. The final step is, there is no other.

Whether you have a capital O or a small o, everything in the last analysis is the divine action. It is happening to you right now, and it is going to continue to happen. All we are asked to do is to accept it. We will know if there is anything we should do in the concrete, and there will be things we are called to do.

How many are your works, O Lord! In wisdom you have
made them all. The earth is full of your riches.
May the glory of the Lord last forever!

PSALM 104:24, 31

two

MEETING GOD

*Think of God in a very big way. So gentle, so consider-
ate, so kind, so tender, so everything marvelous, that is
God. Whatever you say is far less than what is.*

God is in everything, with everything, without being
identified with anything completely. God is always God
and in the extraordinary capacity of this Whatever Is
can be everything in particular and totally present to everything that has been created—yet totally free not to
be. That means free to be you and not to be you. But,
the fact that you are here suggests that God wanted to be
you, wanted to experience human nature in your uniqueness and to manifest in your life and death and whatever
is after your death, and wanted your total openness to
becoming God, too.

I cannot explain how marvelous a concept this is because everything really points to God—and some things
are better than others—and everything is not God any
more than it is God. It is because God is everything at
once! Whenever you say anything positive about God,

unless you say something the same way negatively, you are not talking about the God who is, who was, and who is to come. Since we are locked into rational consciousness at this point, and the spiritual journey is meant to move us on by becoming transpersonal or trans-rational and united with That Which Is, we cannot resolve the apparent opposites of rational consciousness.

If something is something, it cannot be its opposite—or so it might seem. Not so with God, because God is at a place of knowledge and love that is beyond opposites—where all opposites are complementary. In the simplicity of God, everything is resolved. It is into that unity of consciousness that God is inviting us in our human adventure.

Please remember that this God I'm talking about using Judeo-Christian jargon is adventurous and playful. This is a serious thing—becoming God, too—but it has its lighter side. If you miss that, you will risk slipping into a certain inflexibility, or essentialism, or lack of humanity, or at the very least, a lack of humor. Without humor, there is no real sanctity.

Reality could be all a game, as the Hindus say, or it could be a joke. It is all of those things and more—that is the difficulty. Once we get a good idea, we settle into it with all our strength because we have so few good ideas! That is understandable, but not the whole truth. If you have a sharp enough perception, nothing hides God, even the worst of situations, the most stupid of people, and even yourself. This thinking of God I am offering to you is a kind of fireside chat—it is fun.

Think of God in a very big way. And, if you do, that is too small. You cannot think of anything more wonderful than this God. You cannot figure out anything about God without a special grace. The stages that I reduced to three have many sub-stages in between as you climb this staircase or hopefully take the elevator to the top floor—and there is one. It does not depend on you, of course. God is so marvelously good.

There's no word for it. So gentle, so considerate, so kind, so tender, so everything marvelous—that is God. Whatever you say is far less than what is. As Paul says, It hasn't crossed the imagination of any human being what God has prepared. for those who love him (1 Corinthians 2:9).

What else is there to do? You cannot do more for anyone than to love, as the Scripture suggests—totally, with your whole mind, heart, soul, and strength. The Dalai Lama calls this *compassion*. It includes everybody, as in the Second Commandment.

Basically, the Buddhists and the Christians are saying largely the same thing in many respects. They are responding to the desperate need of humans for happiness, which none of them know how to attain.

Even when someone tells you, you do not get it until you try it out and rely more and more on God. Now, I'd like to encourage you that if you have been practicing

Centering Prayer for some years, you are much further along than you can imagine because God is drawing you and is the source of that very sophisticated psychological way in which God draws you irresistibly while giving you complete freedom. If you can put those things together, you will be becoming God, too.

God knows everything that is wrong with you. It does not bother God at all. God rather expects it! This is the great mistake of the Creator, if I may be so bold: to create anything because anything that God creates cannot be perfect. Otherwise, it would be God. God is making a problem for Godself just by making anything. It is going to have faults and all of the rest of the things—it's going to be a mess, a terrible mess!

If you want others to be happy, practice compassion.

If you want to be happy, practice compassion.

HIS HOLINESS THE 14TH DALAI LAMA

three

FRIENDS WITH THE UNIVERSE

As the Fathers of the Church said: there are two books of revelation. One is the Bible, the other is nature. The sub-atomic chaos that we hear about from the astronomers is a good symbol of who we all are.

We're all just a mess! That is to say, at some level, we're just this amazing combination of trillions of sub-atomic particles that are put together by the genius of nature or the evolutionary process, and those little sub-atomic particles are roughly as far away from each other as the galaxies proportionately. That means you and I sitting here are mostly space—a little wind would blow us all away. Who's holding you together? This is a mystery. How are your bosons? These are the new discoveries that are supposed to change spiritual energy or invisible energy into material things.

This is an extraordinary discovery. You and I are on the verge of scientific discoveries that were just unimaginable 20, 30, 40 years ago—unimaginable, and becoming more extraordinary.

What will that do to medicine, the genome, all the other things? What's happening with evolution is that human nature, with its achievement of rational consciousness, is now taking over the co-creation of the universe, at least on this planet. But because everything is inter-related, whatever we do here affects everything else in the universe as it expands at millions of miles an hour. We must not think of this God as picayune.

Put your mind on it: billions of stars in one galaxy, billions of galaxies in the observable universe.

Right now, as we sit here, a supernova that exploded a million years ago and sent forth the last parts of its elementary particles to build new planets and—God only knows—affects everything in the universe is just arriving. You are just being penetrated at this moment by some neuron or something that was exploded a few million, or maybe a billion, years ago. Everything is extremely well thought out without appearing to be so. We may not be able to grow unless some supernova explodes somewhere and shares with us the residue of its enormous energies.

We must begin to be friends with the universe in a way that we never were before because the biblical cosmology represented the cultural, scientific knowledge of its time, which was close to zero compared to where we are now. The predictions of the early Fathers of the Church are now happening, and the revelation of God's inner nature and plans and activities are available to us in new ways that they have never been known before. As the Fathers of the Church said, there are two books of revelation—one is the Bible, the other is nature. Now, nature is not just a beautiful sunset—although it is. It is also the very awareness of the inner nature of how things are working even in the sub-sub-atomic world, or what energies, which are invisible to us but are very real, are just beginning to be known.

We are like babes in the woods compared to the knowledge that is being unearthed. The cellular structure of all life is virtually the same. Just a little difference in this or that gene, and you have huge differences in the outcome. If we would listen to science—serious science that is thoroughly researched and is as certain as anything is going to get at this level of our knowledge—it is revelation about God. At the same time, we know that our capacities for understanding are very humbling, especially if we rely on past cosmology.

"When we try to pick out anything by itself,
we find it hitched to everything else in the Universe."

JOHN MUIR

four

THE NEW COSMOLOGY, RELIGION AND PATHS TO GOD

All humanity is interdependent, and this is what the mystics have always taught with great vigor.

Now science comes along in a completely irreligious culture and discovers the truth that everything is coming from one source, and it is evolving.

Theology itself is struggling in our day from the death of the cosmology, formed about a thousand years before Christ, in which most of the world religions were founded and the great spiritual literature was written. It is out of date. People cannot be expected to be impressed with belief systems that rely on a cosmology that everybody knows does not exist. These are huge problems for the churches, religions, theologians, sociologists, psychologists, and everybody else. There has to be an acceptance and an embracing of dialogue between the wisdom of science and the wisdom of revelation. The wisdom of mystics, which has always been rejected, is just now proving itself to have been centuries ahead of its time.

God has always been God, and the energies have always functioned according to God's will. More and more about the workings of the universe and beyond are beginning to become known because of the technological achievements of the human mind, which is enjoying this vast explosion of information that is getting bigger all the time.

Unfortunately, the vision of life, its value or the value of this information we are receiving, or its meaning, has not made much of a dent on the population as of now. And it will not until the religions of the world take this new science seriously and rethink and re-articulate the mystical wisdom with the facts of science. These two things have to go together.

His Holiness the Dalai Lama, the marvelous witness to compassion and forgiveness—these are Christian virtues, obviously—thinks they belong to human nature and that you could build a common ethic in a world in which religious ethics will never agree in particular. Each one has its own idea, and that is part of its belief system.

His idea is that we accept the human gift that is human nature, which is innately capable of compassion and forgiveness and collaboration, and so on, and begin to practice this and let each society or culture add to this the particulars of its system without denigrating or being disturbed by the differences of other religions as has been the tragic case in the past.

Perhaps no society more than religion itself has done more violence. When violence comes from people who are professing nonviolence, it is a very sad situation. It is a wonder we are still here. Along with the fragility of human nature goes this affirmation of human nature itself. This is a new idea for some theological circles, especially some at the time of the Reformation, who said that human nature is basically evil. Oddly enough, someone asked me the question when I was on the platform with His Holiness [MIT, OCT. 2012]: "Are people basically bad or good in your opinion?" I wasn't expecting this question, but I had to answer. I said, "Well, I understand the Bible says God thought everything was good, especially humans, who are very good. I added, I think it is getting better."

I said that not as a joke but because I really think that we are in an evolutionary process that puts us at the crossroads between our ancestry as animals and our destiny as divine-human beings that God introduced when humankind reached a certain level of rational consciousness, and could reflect on himself and herself, and could appreciate abstract ideas and concepts, and be grateful, and appreciate the good things of creation, and enjoy them.

God did not create us on this planet to be unhappy. God created us with a certain freedom of choice, but that is not what freedom really is. The freedom of choice is limited to various objects. You can choose this and not that. Freedom—the freedom that is perhaps one of the chief aspects of God—is the total freedom to do anything, anytime, anywhere. Freedom is where we are going. Hence, education in how to be free is the most essential part of any curriculum. Freedom as God's gift is another path towards becoming divine yourself. There are many paths. Religion is not the only path to God.

What science is saying now, and this is one of the primary discoveries that has very wide support in the scientific community, which is rare, is that this creation we are in is evolutionary and that it's tarted from a trillionth of a millimeter of energy. Everything, absolutely everything, has come out of that source.

It took millions of years to cool down enough to begin to form just clouds of mist, heat, energy, or whatever was possible, and a very few elements. The way elements come into effect is by the death and resurrection, you might say, of the galaxies or stars. When the star dies, a supernova spews out all the energy that is left at terrific heat, and then it can create new elements. This is how the elements necessary for life gradually took their place in the cosmos over billions of years—13.7 is the date that is given for the moment. Where were you 13 billion years ago? This cosmology is wonderful!

We could not be less significant. The planet is in the middle of nowhere. It is so delicately balanced that any change in a degree or two of this or that, and the whole thing becomes unviable. All humanity is interdependent, and this is what the mystics have always taught with great vigor.

Nobody understood them, of course. Now science comes along in a completely irreligious culture and discovers the truth that everything is coming from one source, and it is evolving.

When evolution reached a certain stage of galaxies and planets, then the necessary elements for life began to appear in one of these deaths of a star, which is very thoroughly cataloged now. A star dies in a certain stage. It is the same death and resurrection scenario that we find in all of life. Everything dies. Everything is born again. Everything remains—the conservation of energy in this planet.

The movement towards becoming rational is there in the evidence everywhere on all the continents, and it is getting more and more numerous—when humans started to speak, when they started to read, when they started to paint the animals they saw around them. Each human being repeats this evolution in our own childhood and developmental growth to the point of adults. We are just animals who think. Rational animals. Rational is only an adjective, the real noun is animal! Please do not think

I am being disrespectful. We are just a bunch of animals still. If you did not have an animal brain, you could not survive more than a few days on this planet. It must be God's will that we have this animal brain that can breathe, that can function instinctively. Perhaps 90% or maybe 95% of all the bodily activities are unconscious to us. We do not have to think about it. We are instinctual on many points just as the animals are. Now, at some point, this instinctual creature, who is simply following his or her nature as an animal, begins to think.

Biologists are saying that human evolution is towards complexity, or all biological development is through complexity. At a certain point, that complexity was complete. This is the point we are at now according to some like Teilhard de Chardin and his cohorts. What does that mean? It means that we are still under the heavy influence of instinctual needs that are in our genes and that our capacity for abstract thinking and human feeling or emotion is completely dependent on our human development, our parental, cultural, and education sources.

If it is God's will to create in an evolutionary manner, which is what science is now saying, then we are only halfway there. We are in the middle of nowhere. We cannot go back to the irresponsibility of the beasts. They follow their instincts, and they glorify God by doing so. We cannot do that anymore because following some of these instincts is a choice, and we have been given freedom of choice by God. Do you think God does not expect us to make mistakes? Is it a good idea to call these mistakes "sins?" Or, might it be better to say, "Sorry, you are a little unevolved?" This is the human condition—seems to have placed us in this transitional state, which, from the perspective of clarity and peaceful growth, is impossible.

You try to do good, and as Paul says very frankly in his famous text, What I want to do, I do not do and what I do not want to do, that's what I do (Romans 7: 15). That is everybody's experience. That is the human condition, and everybody in the world experiences the same thing. Christians, following Saint Augustine, call it original sin.

There are other explanations for this common human experience of not being able to do what you want to do freely.

When you can do what is right freely, this is freedom. Nothing else is freedom. It is a free choice. And because we have free choice, we have the accountability for our free choices and their consequences. God can forgive us all of our failings because God sympathizes with our weaknesses. The consequences of sin are what have been in the forefront of Christian religious understanding for centuries. That does not mean we were wrong but that also may mean we did not have enough information to find a better explanation for our experience.

This is where I think our very idea of God, even if we do not know God, has to change from being guilt-ridden and shame-based, or formed from any other idea that gives us a fear of God, or a negative idea of God, or a lesser understanding of a goodness that is infinite and forgiving. We have been told this over and over again in both Old and New Testaments—more so, of course, much more so, in Jesus' teaching.

―――――――――

*"Grace means that all your mistakes
now serve a purpose instead of serving shame."*

BRENÉ BROWN

five

THE CROSS

What God has done in becoming human is take the lowest place. The lowest place is where you are most likely to find God—in the experience of weakness or rejection. Why? Because God loves us so much.

When you put the cross on a wall without a body, this is the human condition, crucified between heaven and earth. You cannot go back. You cannot go forward under your own power. All you can do is accept the situation and the consequence of failure—no fault of one's own yet—to integrate the instinctual and inevitable needs and demands of nature with the abstract values and meanings that come with human intelligence and freedom of choice with the possibility of ultimate freedom.

This is quite an important concept. You deserve compassion, not condemnation. To think that God would punish people for failing to measure-up in a situation that is impossible or close to impossible is a denigration of the infinite goodness of God. That is why I say you have to have a big idea of God. Maybe God wants to find out what it is like to be human in this situation. Maybe God is so humble that God wishes to make everybody else God, too, as that seems to be the divine-human project if you believe Jesus Christ and the Gifts of the Spirit and Saint Paul's teaching and especially the Priestly Prayer of Jesus when he asked that we all may be one as the Father and I are one (John 17:21).

This is infinite oneness, infinite unity. It is not a number but a state of consciousness in which oneness, whatever that is, is experienced in the now moment. Looking at that cross then could not be more shocking, but that is what all people prior to the time of Jesus were facing. They were experiencing the human condition as weakness, the domination of their tormenting emotions, the result of not being able to integrate love, forgiveness, care, conflict, and violence from an animal reaction to a specifically human one.

Suppose you put a body on that cross. Now you are saying something else—that this person is identifying with and choosing the human condition. This is what God seems to have done. God decided to become totally identified with human nature by taking a complete human nature unto Godself, so to speak. Paul puts it explicitly in Philippians. In the words of that wonderful hymn, The Word of God didn't consider being united to God something to cling to (Philippians 2:6). Who would want to be this human in utter misery or potentially there when you are enjoying the fullness?

In other words, God's humility is what we most have to learn: to be completely at God's disposal and to be willing to be the least of humanity.

As Jesus in his Parables recommended to the Pharisees: Take the last place at table. Be the servant of everyone (Mark 9:35). This is what God has done in becoming human. God took the lowest place, rejected by the religious and cultural authorities and politicians of his time. In other words, the lowest place is where you are most likely to find God—in the experience of weakness or rejection or your own rejection of yourself if nobody else will reject you. Why?

Because God loves us so much. God wants to give us the same joy in being whatever we are, and that may be sinners in our own view. That is why in the Christian tradition, the disposition to bring ourselves to nothingness, or to acknowledge who we are, or to ask forgiveness—this is what life is all about. This is the joy of the Kingdom—to be free of our personal and ambiguous confusions about what happiness is and to allow God in God's infinite wisdom let happen to us what happens.

On the cross, Christ has become, literally, the lowest, the least, and in some respects, the most loathsome of human beings—the greatest failure of all time, humanly speaking. He could have done something else. In fact, he asked that the chalice might pass. What Jesus is showing is the heart of the Father in order to reveal this incredible goodness, charity, compassion, forgiveness, tenderness, and desire to make us enjoy all the same divine qualities and dispositions. This is what God the Father is all about.

God does not give us everything we want,
but He does fulfill His promises,
leading us along the best and straightest paths to Himself.

DIETRICH BONHOEFFER

six

REDEMPTION

Just as cells in the body, the immune cells, heal the diseased cells so to be a living cell in the Body of Christ is ... total self-giving or self-surrender, including the willingness to suffer our slice of the human condition for the love of God and the healing of humanity.

There are other symbols in this extraordinary image of the crucifix: the passion of God to forgive, to bring us back into the unity that we had when we were just a thought in the Divine Mind. This is the cross as the manifestation of God's infinite love for each person. Remember, it is the interdependence of the whole human species that was the foundation physiologically for God becoming human, the universal human being, and to bring us back, not just as a group but as individuals, into the bosom of the Father, so to speak.

Also, in this body on the cross is the symbol of taking away all sin. If there are sins, they are taken away by this identification of God in the Person of the Word with all the consequences of human failure, sin, degradation, and all the rest of it.

But redemption from sin is not the main point. Such was the theology of St. Bonaventure and the Franciscans and of Teilhard de Chardin, which is gaining acceptance today. This theology of the capacity of God to take away all the consequences of sin has always been present but not recognized as warmly as the Thomistic theology of the Middle Ages was. That is really what it means. You take away the sin of the world. It is not paying some debt according to the evolutionary view but is a healing process. It is interesting to note that in the Old Testament, salvation and redemption are used almost exclusively for healing or for escaping, like the escape from Egypt, which is called redemption.

There needs to be an adjustment of understanding—or at least an understanding of equal force—of the marvelous theology of Bonaventure, in which the purpose of Christ's Passion and Death is not primarily to take away sin—that's an obvious consequence—but to invite us to become divine, too. It's saying, I'll do anything, anything, to convince you of my love for you and desire to share all that I am with you—insofar as that is possible within the human container, even when it's been expanded by every grace.

Once you accept redemption from sin as a byproduct, the cross takes on this enormously positive aspect and becomes the symbol of an absolutely open invitation to become God, too, insofar as that's possible. If you're thinking of becoming a saint, I give you credit, but it is too low! When you are invited to become divine, you do not have to worry about becoming a saint.

This is perhaps one of the great meanings of the myth of Adam and Eve. It is not history.

The early writers of the scriptures did not know how to write history in the critical sense that we understand it. They used myth to communicate truth as they saw it. Adam and Eve are invited to divine union. This trial, if that is what it is, is to give them a chance to deserve it or to make it on their own. They are given every possibility to freely accept it.

Satan, whoever he is, comes along—maybe it is our unconscious. (There is plenty of scientific evidence for some malevolent influences at work here.) Hear what Jesus seems to be saying in the Scriptures: I want you to become God, too, but on my terms, because these are the only ones that will work." Satan comes along and says, "You can become God but on your own terms. That is the ultimate question of religion. For all of us, at some point, our desire for happiness is confronted by this question: Do you want to become God on your own terms? You will not make it, because there is no such path. If you want to become God on God's terms by doing God's will and loving God completely, it is all open territory. It is all yours.

There is one last aspect to this extraordinary meaning to Christian life that the Passion and Death of Jesus projects from the cross and that is, Would you like to join me in this project? In other words, Would you want to co-redeem with me to heal humanity by virtue of your place, accepted by Baptism and in your life? Would you be willing to share the sufferings of humanity, of the human condition, with me so as to heal the members of this Mystical Body? How about it? It is an invitation.

The Buddhists have this in their teaching, too. The Bodhisattvas are those who are willing, although they have attained enlightenment, to be the last ones to enjoy its fruits. They wait until everybody else has gone in first, which is really what Jesus has done. He has gone first into hell. That is why the descent into hell is so important. To me, it is the final stage or expression or manifestation of what God has done in Christ, which is to become sin. You remember Paul said, "He who knew not sin was made sin (2 Corinthians 5:21).

That is, Christ was placed in the full human condition that we experience without being able to do much about it. It is an extraordinary expression of love. In other words, when you join me in descending into hell, you help release the prisoners of the consequences of their unevolved situation. Just as cells in the body, the immune cells, heal the diseased cells that are there, so to be a living cell in the Body of Christ is to have the same dispositions of total self-giving or self-surrender, including the willingness to suffer our slice of the human condition for the love of God and the healing of humanity.

We are accountable to everybody else. What you do, I do. What you are doing, your virtue, I can claim. I can also burden you with my vices. Everything is in common.

"Contrary to what we may have been taught to think, unnecessary and unchosen suffering wounds us but need not scar us for life. It does mark us. What we allow the mark of our suffering to become is in our own hands."

bell hooks

seven

PARTICIPATING IN THE DIVINE LIFE

Contemplative knowing is this inter-penetration of spirits with God in which human nature and the divine nature are intermingled and become one, and the oneness turns out to be everything. So to become nothing in oneself is to become everything in What Is. This will change the world.

We have to expand our understanding of God's goodness and our own capacity. In other words, affirm from the bottom of our heart our own goodness as created by God, the image and likeness of God, and the capacity to become God, too, through divine grace.

Peter defines grace as a participation in the divine life (2 Peter 1:4). To look at Christ dying on the cross is to look at his invitation to join him in total self-sacrifice for the healing and transformation of the whole human race and the realization, as the Book of Revelation says, of the New Creation and the New Earth. In this somewhat comprehensive view, the whole Christian life and revelation, as we know it, is put before us in terms that are perhaps different in emphasis from what we might have learned in our catechisms and theology books. It is partially due to the service of science; some scientists are probably prophets of the new humanity.

Suppose that you take the hand of Jesus and Mary, so to speak, and offer to descend into hell as a psychological state. Lots of people are in hell right now while living among us and maybe you have been there too a few times. It may not be eternal yet. You know your nothingness, and you know your capacity for all evil, and you know your invitation to become divine, and they are all mixed up in a single psychological experience of utter powerlessness. Congratulations! You finally got there— that is to say, you have finally become a totally healthy cell in the Mystical Body. What happens to you next?

That is God's secret, but you do not care, because to love God and to do God's will is what heaven is. Perhaps the best description of heaven is to do good all day long. If you are doing that, you do not need any other ascesis. However, I do not think you will make it there unless you meditate and do contemplative prayer. I think what the church suffers from today is the lack of contemplatives.

Without a significant number of people who are exposing themselves to the divine love without intermediaries, you will not know what the right thing to do is. You will not have the perspective, the tasting, that the divine Presence even very elementally brings into your life.

Many have had the experience of non-duality, reconciliation or affirmation of your goodness. You know that God is loving you and you know that is not a trick. It is because you are lovable. You are the image of God. You are called to enter the bosom of the Father. You are called to identification with Jesus in this life, and that means to identify also with sinners, with yourself, as a sinner. With everybody you are identifying with compassion, not judgment, and with humility, not domination. Authority comes from Being, not from position.

We need authority but that comes from servant leadership. In Christianity, there is not any genuine leadership without it being service.

Through Centering Prayer, you will be given that perspective without thinking. It just happens. It is our deepest nature. The false self has to go, and the Night of Sense takes care of that. The ego has to go. Night of Spirit will take care of that. The transcendent self or the true Self begins to come in focus not through words but by the silence of interior prayer becoming Presence. You cannot describe it. You just know that it is so.

Just as Adam and Eve knew each other and conceived their children, so contemplative knowing is this inter-penetration of spirits—the conjugal relationship, you might say, with God, in which human nature and the divine nature are intermingled and become one, and the oneness turns out to be everything, so that to become nothing in oneself is to become everything in What Is. This will change the world. I doubt if anything else will do so. The hours of boredom and of having to deal with the distractions that you do not want—do not pay any attention to that. It is just a part of the human condition.

Ignore it. Let it all pass.

The thoughts that come—and allow whatever thoughts to come into your mind—give Jesus a chance to take care of them or to find out what you are thinking about or to deliver you from paying any attention to them. Resist not evil, he says in the Sermon on the Mount (Matthew 5:39). If you regard distractions as an evil, or you fight them, then you get involved with them. Just treat them as the usual parade that passes through our minds. With time, they will diminish and perhaps disappear. Opening to God is not effort. Do not try too hard, or do not have a particular goal, as we cannot imagine how good is what God wants to give us.

"I pray to the birds because they remind me
of what I love rather than what I fear.
And at the end of my prayers,
they teach me how to listen."

TERRY TEMPEST WILLIAMS

eight

ALL IN ALL

Be still and you will know not by the knowledge of the mind but by the knowledge of the heart who God is and who you are.

Finally, just a few words about the way this Beloved functions: you can have any relationship you want with God. As a Christian, we might think of a relationship with Jesus Christ because this more than any other truth of our faith makes the relationship personal. Our brothers and sisters in the East never had to develop a theological understanding of person or what we mean by person. For the first time in history, the new dialogue that is possible through scientific progress, travel, and communications, enables long-experienced practitioners of different spiritual traditions to come together. These groups are called different things. We have such a group at Snowmass called the Snowmass Interspiritual Conference, which is a dialogue between people who embody various spiritual traditions.

If we could just let God act, and trust about a million times more than we do now, we cannot believe in God's love to excess because we cannot come near to comprehending the magnitude of this love. Whatever constitutes the passion of love in God is so great and powerful. We cannot imagine what it is, but we can experience a taste of it, which is transforming, and this taste will become stronger as we get closer to death. If it gets too strong, of course, you are going to die.

It is too powerful to endure. It is like finding yourself in a furnace. If you do not turn it down in a hurry, you will not last much longer.

Prayer and activity are not enemies. We ascend the ladder of consciousness beyond rational consciousness to intuitive and unitive levels, and then, when they become stabilized, action and contemplation become the same thing because God is present in everything. You see God in everything, and you see God intentionally working with circumstances outside of you and inside of you to teach you something new.

Sometimes this teaching is about your faults. You see you still have an attachment to ambition or fame or applause or all those other egoic-self projects. It is not that they are all going to go away, but they become powerless to influence you anymore. It is just the human condition...blah, blah, let it go.

Everything bothers you and nothing bothers you at the same time. Everything bothers you because you are so sensitive and compassionate to everybody's pain. You wish you could help them, and you do not seem to be able to, and maybe God is not asking you to. The absolutely certain help you can give to someone else is to work on yourself—that is, by loving more, becoming more humble, by trusting more. You do not usually have to do anything else, and that will save you a lot of useless trouble. Yes, God will inspire you to particular things, but you do not worry about the results or the success or lack of it. It is love that is doing the work, and as it becomes purified, it becomes the immaculate love.

The Blessed Mother, Jesus, the Father, and the Holy Spirit are constantly and infinitely giving to each other and inviting us into the same stream of consciousness and bliss. I do hope that being together, you will receive the strength that each of you has achieved in your personal efforts, which is communicable.

I do not know how it works, but when a group of like-minded people committed to the transformative processes are together, the force of the energy is certainly up a number of decibels higher. You do not have to do anything but be still and let your mind be quiet. Know that God's word is spoken fully only in silence. Be still, and you will know, not by the knowledge of the mind, but by the knowledge of the heart, who God is and who you are.

"You'll never find me. For I have been with you, from the beginning of me."

JALAL AL-DIN MUHAMMAD RUMI

FURTHER REFLECTIONS BY THOMAS KEATING

If you want to pray ...

Centering Prayer responds to this invitation:

i. by consenting to God's presence and action within

ii. by surrendering our will completely to God

iii. by relating to God who dwells in secret,
which is the silence of self.

...

As God brings the new creation to life in interior
silence, that is to say, the new you, the worldview that
Christ shares in deep silence becomes more important
than our own. Then God asks us to live that new life
in the circumstances of everyday life, contradicted by
turmoil, opposition and anxieties of all kinds.

OPEN MIND, OPEN HEART

Contemplative prayer is a process of interior
transformation, a conversion initiated by God and
leading, if we consent to divine union.

One's way of seeing reality changes in this process.
A restructuring of consciousness takes place which
empowers one to perceive, relate and respond
to everyday life with increasing sensitivity
to the divine Presence in, through
and beyond everything that happens.

OPEN MIND, OPEN HEART

———

Bonding with others takes place as the love
of the Spirit is poured forth in our hearts.
We feel that we belong to our community,
to the human family, to the cosmos. We feel
that our prayer is not just a privatized journey but is
having a significant effect in the world.

We can pour into the world the love
that the Spirit gives us in prayer.

INTIMACY WITH GOD

Under the influence of the Holy Spirit ... our actions
are more and more emerging from that place
of surrender, silence and receptivity that is
the full development of the contemplative process.

HEARTFULNESS: TRANSFORMATION IN CHRIST

———

If one is transformed, one can walk down the street,
drink a cup of tea or shake hands with somebody and be
pouring divine life into the world. Transmission is the
capacity to awaken in other people their own potential-
ity to become divine.

THE MYSTERY OF CHRIST

———

We are called to this journey not just
for our own personal growth, but also for
the sake of the whole human community.

INVITATION TO LOVE

What Matters

Only the Divine Matters,
And because the Divine matters,

Everything matters.

THE SECRET EMBRACE

———

May God bless you all the days of your life.

Amen.

_____

THOMAS KEATING MEMORIAL MASS NOVEMBER 15, 2018

BY CARL J. ARICO

Thank you in a very special way for loving Father Thomas as we all do. For we are not just loving Thomas, we are loving Christ in Thomas who connects in the Christness within each one of us.

Since we received the news of Thomas' death on October 25, 2018, I am sure we thought of our own lives. I am going to ask you three questions: Since that time, what have we become aware of that needs to be forgiven in our own lives? What have we become aware of that needs to be healed in our lives? What have we become aware of that needs to be celebrated more in our lives?

In that spirit, let us begin: In the name of the Father and of the Son and of the Holy Spirit, Amen. We pray almighty God for the soul of your servant Thomas, who, for love of Christ walked the way of perfect charity. May he rejoice in the coming of your glory, and together with his brothers and his sisters and all the loved ones that he cherished in his life, may he delight in the everlasting happiness of your Kingdom, through our Lord Jesus Christ, your Son, who lives and reigns with you in the unity of the Holy Spirit. One God forever and ever, Amen.

Jesus said to his disciples, Do not let your hearts be troubled. You have faith in God, have faith also in me. In my Father's house, there are many dwelling places. If there were not, would I have told you that I am going to prepare a place for you? And if I go and prepare a place for you, I will come back again and take you to myself so that where I am you also may be. Where I am going you know the way. Thomas said to him, Master, we do not know where you are going. How can we know the way?"

Jesus said to him, I am the way, the truth and the life, no one comes to the Father except through me (John 14:1-6). The Gospel of the Lord.

No one ever spoke as this man (John 7:46). Another translation, We have never heard anyone speak like this. These words for me capture the essence of Father Thomas Keating's gift to us: No one ever spoke as this man.

It was not only his words, but it was his presence. I would sit there for an hour and listen to him and when he was complete, I would say, Wow, that was beautiful! That was powerful! Then if someone asked me, What did he say?" I would say, "Well, I don't know what he said, but it was right on. It was meaningful. And you are still learning something from them, so no one speaks as that man speaks.

I was thinking of some things he said that we will never forget:

The only thing you can do wrong in Centering Prayer is to get up and leave.

All I can say is persevere.

Silence is God's first language. Everything else is a poor translation.

When we say, Let us pray, we are saying, Let us have a relationship.

You know, the false self does not drop dead on command.

Lectio Divina is like a heavy date with God.

Power and control, affection and esteem, security and survival—those are the energy centers we need to deal with. (And that is true. They are still in each one of us, even with those who have been journeying with Thomas for over 40 years. They are still there.)

Centering prayer is the perfect preparation for death because one has already died to the false self.

Our basic core of goodness is our true Self. Its

center of gravity is God. The acceptance or the embracing of our basic goodness is a quantum leap in the spiritual journey.

Down is up and up is down, so you cannot humble yourself without being exalted and you cannot exalt yourself without being humbled.

To know the Other, to become the Other. There is no Other.

No one ever spoke as this man does. We have never heard anyone speak like this. He was gifted because he consented to God's presence and action in his life. If he did not teach us to consent to God's presence and action on a much deeper level than we had been aware of, we would not be experiencing the same things in ourselves because we are beloved. We are made in the image and likeness of God."

Each one of us remembers Thomas in a different way. I invite you to close your eyes for a few moments. When I say the name Father Thomas Keating, what do you picture? What do you experience, what do you remember when you hear the name Father Thomas Keating? Hold on to that, embrace that because each one of us is a piece of a mosaic that reflects his presence, his influence, his impact on each of us and on our world. He was like a flower that grew and bloomed and as a flower, he stayed in himself. In his death, the seeds from that flower have gone out to each one of us and beyond. That seed can grow if the ground keeps open to the watering of the Holy Spirit and each one of us can flower, bloom and do what needs to be done to continue the unbelievable Christian tradition of the resting and consenting to God's presence and action in our lives.

When I heard that Father Joseph had died and then soon after when I heard that Father Thomas had died, this is the image that struck me: Joseph went to prepare the way because, to be honest with you, Thomas liked to have the way prepared for him. Joseph went to prepare the way and Thomas joined him and the image I had was the disciples on the way to Emmaus. Joseph waited, Thomas came, Jesus met them, and Jesus then straightened out both of them on their walk to Emmaus where they sat down and enjoyed the companionship that they had from the moment they were conceived.

Why did Thomas end up dying in Spencer and not Snowmass? That is a mystery that people are wondering. Well, I will throw in my two cents: he had to go home where it all began to complete the circle. It was in Rhode Island and Spencer, Massachusetts that his vocation began to grow. He had to be reborn; he had to finish his unfinished business and allow himself to be loved again where it all began.

When I visited him the first time [at St. Joseph's] at

the beginning of July, Thomas was there and Gail Fitzpatrick-Hopler came to visit too. I wanted to be with him in a way that I was with my father when he was dying, so I asked him, Thomas, can I pray with you like I prayed with my dad when he was dying? Like my family prayed with him when he was dying?" He said, "Yes, yes." My father's favorite prayer, as he was ending his life, was the Prayer of Abandonment which we prayed during the last two or three days of his life. Now, when we were all done, he said, "Could I have that prayer?" I handed it to him, not knowing what was going to happen.

We went to visit again in the middle of September. This time he looked at me and he said, Will you say that prayer?" I said, "Which one?" "The prayer you gave me." I prayed it and then I heard later from Abbott Damien that almost every time he went in to visit Thomas, Thomas would say to him, Pray this prayer with me. Pray this prayer with me.

What a privilege it was to tuck my father into God's arms and to be part of tucking my spiritual father into God's arms 40 years later. Somehow, I feel that that prayer is Thomas last will and testament to us because he never taught us any other prayer. He taught us how to pray but I never recall him teaching us a prayer in our time together. I really also think that the prayer captured what was going on in his heart as he was going through the final purification before going to the God he loved. I also feel it captures what consent is all about especially when we enter into Centering Prayer:

Father, I abandon myself into your hands; do with me what you will.

Whatever you may do, I thank you. I am ready for all, I accept all.

Let only your will be done in me and in all your creatures.

I wish no more than this, O Lord. Into your hands I commend my soul;

I offer to you with all the love of my heart, for I love you, Lord and so need to give myself,

to surrender myself into your hands without reserve and with confidence for you are my Father. Amen.

-CHARLES DE FOUCAULD

We pray, O Lord, that the soul of our brother, Thomas, to whom you gave a part in your covenant, may be purified by the power of this mystery and rejoice without end in the peace of Christ who lives and reigns forever and ever. Amen.

THOMAS KEATING MEMORIAL MASS
NOVEMBER 15, 2018

BY TED JONES, NEPHEW

———

highlights

Today, as we celebrate the life of Father Thomas Keating and also mourn his death, it is surely worth reflecting on the accomplishments of this extraordinary human being: his leadership in interspiritual dialogue among the world's great religious traditions, the millions of people throughout the world whose lives he touched and enriched through his books and his ministry of Centering Prayer, and the founding of Contemplative Outreach, a spiritual organization, international in scope to which we owe thanks for this beautiful service here today.

What is more important to remember about Father Thomas is that he took credit for none of this. I am going to read now some of his own words from the book, From the *Mind to the Heart*:

Most of my life, I failed in all the things I wanted to do or hope to accomplish. Coming to terms with that very existential experience is what I regard as my greatest treasure. I will put it in one word, powerlessness. Success is one of the most dangerous of all human experiences especially in religious circles.

The higher stages of the transformative process are so wonderful that the temptation to attribute this transformation to ourselves is very strong. In fact, the temptation is so dangerous that God, in his great love for us, makes sure that we do not run the risk of attributing any of our accomplishments to ourselves. The tendency to take possession of our accomplishments is the chief obstacle to divine transformation and it is called pride.

Father Thomas fully realized an essential truth of the spiritual journey: that in the end, nothing is claimed. It is not our will but God's that has been done.

Father Thomas was my uncle. His sister, the late Anne Keating Jones, was my mother. They were close as children and they remained close throughout their lives. My relationship with Father Thomas really began in my early 20s at the beginning of a haphazard search for my own spiritual path. I clearly remember a phone conversation I had with him during this period. At the time, I was dabbling in TM, Transcendental Meditation, and he asked me how often I was meditating. I replied with a convoluted justification for why I thought it was a good idea just to meditate whenever I felt like it. His response betrayed no judgment whatsoever; it was just a simple statement of fact, Well, you have to do it every day.

His directness left me speechless, but it propelled me toward a daily meditation practice that has continued ever since. I eventually found my spiritual path in the Buddhist practice of Insight Meditation, also known as Vipassana. Despite our immersion in different traditions, Father Thomas continued to be very helpful to me. During one period of intensive practice when my teacher was away on a six-month retreat, I leaned heavily on him as a resource. His encouragement and guidance were invaluable.

Over the years, we remained in contact, but it was not until my retirement eight years ago that our relationship began to really flourish again. With time to deepen my practice, I found more and more common ground with him. We began to spend more time together and have long conversations on the phone.

The memory that I hold most dear is just the person that he was—what it was like to spend time with him, to experience his love, his sense of humor, his humility and his boundless devotion to God. When he moved back to Spencer last spring, I became the relative living closest to him, about an hour and a half away.

On September 25th, I received a call that he was near death and not expected to live more than two or three days. I visited him the next morning. He was glad to see me but very weak. I returned the next day and stayed at the monastery overnight, uncertain if he would be alive the next morning. Father Thomas survived that night and continued to survive day by day. I began spending as much time as I could with him, staying at the monastery three to four nights a week. Most of that time was just spent sitting silently at his bedside.

On October 13th, 17 days after that initial call, I was scheduled to lead a day-long retreat at the meditation center where I have a small teaching role. The title of that retreat was Insight Meditation and Christian Spiritual Practice which I was presenting along with a Methodist minister. Father Thomas and I had discussed the idea and planning for this retreat a number of times. He had been very encouraging and happy that I was doing it. As the day of the retreat drew near, I was quite conflicted about whether to cancel it. Ultimately, I decided to go ahead, believing that even if Father Thomas died that day, I would be doing something that he cared about passionately and that I would be contributing in some small way to his legacy.

Before I left, he was strong enough for a brief conversation. I told him I was leaving to teach at the retreat and that I would be holding him in my heart throughout the day. He thanked me and said he was pleased. The retreat was no big deal, but it was meaningful for those who were there. About a dozen of us spent most of the day in silent meditation and prayer with the discussion of how these two traditions could complement one another along the spiritual journey.

I began the day by reading some of Father Thomas words and ended the retreat the same way. Afterwards, three or four people approached me and asked if they could have a copy of what I had just read. One person said to me, Please personally thank your uncle for me. When I returned to the monastery the next day, Father Thomas condition had slipped, and It seemed that no conversation would be possible. His eyes were closed, and he was unresponsive when I greeted him. I felt sad as I stood by his bed but spoke anyway, describing the retreat just as I have to you.

When I had finished, he opened his eyes slightly and said, That's wonderful. I'm going to end by reading the passage that I read at the conclusion of that retreat, From the *Mind to the Heart*, chapter five. At the end of the reading, we'll have a few moments of silence.

The world desperately needs people free of cultural allusions and who are undertaking a dedicated exploration of true reality. Not just to know the material nature of things, but also to know the very Source of everything that exists.

An unfolding contemplative practice eventually becomes total receptivity. In that receptivity, one is aware of a silence that is becoming an irresistible attraction. Silence leads to stillness, stillness leads to surrender.

While this doesn't happen every time we sit down to pray, interior silence gradually opens to an inner spaciousness that is alive. In this context, if we speak of emptiness, we are not speaking of just emptiness, but of emptiness that is beginning to be filled with a Presence.

Perhaps we could say that contemplation occurs when interior silence morphs into Presence. This Presence, once established in our innermost being, might be called spaciousness. There is nothing in it except a certain vibrancy and aliveness. You are awake but awake to what you don't know. You are awake to something you cannot describe and which is absolutely marvelous, totally generous and which manifests itself with increasing tenderness, sweetness and intimacy.

Amen.

GUIDELINES FOR CHRISTIAN LIFE, GROWTH & TRANSFORMATION

FROM OPEN MIND, OPEN HEART

The following principles represent a tentative effort to restate the Christian spiritual journey in contemporary terms. They are designed to provide a conceptual background for the practice of Centering Prayer. They should be read according to the method of Lectio Divina.

1. The fundamental goodness of human nature, like the mystery of the Trinity, Grace and the Incarnation, is an essential element of Christian faith. This basic core of goodness is capable of unlimited development; indeed, of becoming transformed into Christ and deified.

2. Our basic core of goodness is our true Self. Its center of gravity is God. The acceptance of our basic goodness is a quantum leap in the spiritual journey.

3. God and our true Self are not separate. Though we are not God, God and our true Self are the same thing.

4. The term original sin is a way of describing the human condition, which is the universal experience of coming to full reflective self-consciousness without the certitude of union with God. This gives rise to our intimate sense of incompletion, dividedness, isolation and guilt.

5. Original sin is not the result of personal wrongdoing on our part. Still, it causes a pervasive feeling of alienation from God, from other people and from the true Self. The cultural consequences of these alienations are instilled in us from earliest childhood and passed on from one generation to the next. The urgent need to escape from the profound insecurity of this situation gives rise, when unchecked, to insatiable desires for pleasure, possession and power. On the social level, it gives rise to violence, war and institutional injustice.

6. The consequences of original sin include all the self-serving habits that have been woven into our personality from the time we were conceived; all the emotional damage that has come from our early environment and upbringing; all the harm that other people have done to us knowingly or unknowingly at an age when we could not defend ourselves; and the methods we acquired—many of them now unconscious—to ward off the pain of unbearable situations.

7. This constellation of pre-rational reactions is the foundation of the false self. The false self develops in opposition to the true Self. Its center of gravity is itself.

8. Grace is the presence and action of Christ at every moment of our lives. The sacraments are ritual actions in which Christ is present in a special manner, confirming and sustaining the major commitments of our Christian life.

9. In Baptism, the false self is ritually put to death, the new self is born and the victory over sin won by Jesus through his death and Resurrection is placed at our disposal. Not our uniqueness as persons, but our sense of separation from God and from others is destroyed in the death-dealing and life-giving waters of Baptism.

10. The Eucharist is the celebration of life: the coming together of all the material elements of the cosmos, their emergence to consciousness in human persons, and the transformation of human consciousness into divine consciousness. It is the manifestation of the Divine in and through the Christian community. We receive the Eucharist in order to become the Eucharist.

11. In addition to being present in the sacraments, Christ is present in a special manner in every crisis and important event of our lives.

12. Personal sin is the refusal to respond to Christ's self-communication (grace). It is the deliberate neglect of our own genuine needs and those of others. It reinforces the false self.

13. Our basic core of goodness is dynamic and tends to grow of itself. This growth is hindered by the illusions and emotional hang-ups of the false self, by the negative influences coming from our cultural conditioning, and by personal sin.

14. Listening to God's word in Scripture and the liturgy, waiting upon God in prayer, and responsiveness to his inspirations help to distinguish how the two selves are operating in particular circumstances.

15. God is not some remote, inaccessible, and implacable Being who demands instant perfection from his creatures and of whose love we must make ourselves worthy. He is not a tyrant to be obeyed out of terror, nor a policeman who is ever on the watch, nor a harsh judge ever ready to apply the verdict of guilty. We should relate to him less and less in terms of reward and punishment

and more and more on the basis of the gratuity—or the play—of divine love.

16. Divine love is compassionate, tender, luminous, totally self-giving, seeking no reward, unifying everything.

17. The experience of being loved by God enables us to accept our false self as it is, and then to let go of it and journey to our True Self. The inward journey to our true Self is the way to divine love.

18. The growing awareness of our true Self, along with the deep sense of spiritual peace and joy which f low from this experience, balances the psychic pain of the disintegrating and dying of the false self. As the motivating power of the false self diminishes, our true Self builds the new self with the motivating force of the divine love.

19. The building of our new self is bound to be marked by innumerable mistakes and sometimes by sin. Such failures, however serious, are insignificant compared to the inviolable goodness of our true Self. We should ask God's pardon, seek forgiveness from those we may have offended, and then act with renewed confidence and energy as if nothing had happened.

20. Prolonged, pervasive, or paralyzing guilt feelings come from the false self. True guilt in response to personal sin or social injustice does not lead to discouragement but to amendment of life. It is a call to conversion.

21. Progress in the spiritual journey is manifested by the unconditional acceptance of other people, beginning with those with whom we live.

22. A community of faith offers the support of example, correction and mutual concern in the spiritual journey. Above all, participating in the mystery of Christ through the celebration of the liturgy, praying the scriptures and silent prayer binds the community in a common search for transformation and union with God. The presence of Christ is ministered to each other and becomes tangible in the community, especially when it is gathered for worship or engaged in some work of service to those in need.

23. The moderation of the instinctual drives of the developing human organism for survival and security, affection and esteem, control and power allows true human needs to come into proper focus. Primary among these needs is intimacy with another or several human persons. By intimacy is meant the mutual self-disclosure of thoughts, feelings, problems and spiritual aspirations which gradually develops into spiritual friendship.

24. Spiritual friendship involving genuine self-disclosure is an essential ingredient for happiness both in marriage and in the celibate lifestyle. The experience of intimacy with another or several persons expands and deepens our capacity to relate to God and to everyone else. Under the influence of divine love the sexual energy is gradually transformed into universal compassion.

25. The spiritual radiation of a community depends on the commitment of its members to the transformational journey and to each other. To offer one another space in which to grow as persons is an integral part of this commitment.

26. Contemplative prayer, in the traditional sense of the term, is the dynamic that initiates, accompanies and brings the process of transformation to completion.

27. Reflection on the Word of God in Scripture and in our personal history is the foundation of Centering Prayer. The spontaneous letting go of particular thoughts and feelings in prayer is a sign of progress. Centering Prayer is characterized not so much by the absence of thoughts and feelings as by detachment from them.

28. The goal of genuine spiritual practice is not the rejection of the good things of the body, mind, or spirit, but the right use of them. No aspect of human nature or period of human life is to be rejected but integrated into

each successive level of unfolding self-consciousness. In this way, the partial goodness proper to each stage of human development is preserved and only its limitations are left behind. The way to become divine is thus to become fully human.

29. The practice of a spiritual discipline is essential at the beginning of the spiritual journey as a means of developing the foundations of the contemplative dimension of life: dedication and devotion to God and service to others.

30. Regular periods of silence and solitude quiet the psyche, foster interior silence and initiate the dynamic of self-knowledge.

31. Solitude is not primarily a place but an attitude of total commitment to God. When one belongs completely to God, the sharing of one's life and gifts continually increases.

32. The beatitude of poverty of spirit springs from the increasing awareness of our True Self. It is a non-possessive attitude toward everything and a sense of unity with everything at the same time. The interior freedom to have much or to have little and the simplifying of one's lifestyle are signs of the presence of poverty of spirit.

33. Chastity is distinct from celibacy, which is the commitment to abstain from the genital expression of our sexuality. Chastity is the acceptance of our sexual energy together with the masculine and feminine qualities that accompany it, and the integration of this energy into our spirituality. It is the practice of moderation and self-control in the use of sexual energy.

34. Chastity enhances and expands the power to love. It perceives the sacredness of everything that is. As a consequence, one respects the dignity of other persons and cannot use them merely for one's own fulfillment.

35. Obedience is the unconditional acceptance of God as he is and as he manifests himself in our lives. God's will is not immediately evident. Docility inclines us to attend to all the indications of his will. Discernment sifts the evidence and then decides, in the light of the inward attraction of grace, what God seems to be asking here and now.

36. Humility is an attitude of honesty with God, oneself, and all reality. It enables us to be at peace in the presence of our powerlessness and to rest in the forgetfulness of self.

37. Hope springs from the continuing experience of God's compassion and help. Patience is hope in action. It waits for the saving help of God without giving up, giving in, or going away.

38. The disintegrating and dying of our false self is our participation in the passion and death of Jesus. The building of our new self, based on the transforming power of divine love, is our participation in his risen life.

39. In the beginning, emotional hand-ups are the chief obstacle to the growth of our new self because they put our freedom into a straight jacket. Later, because of the subtle satisfaction that springs from self-control, spiritual pride becomes the chief obstacle. And finally, reflection of self becomes the chief obstacle because this hinders the innocence of divine union.

40. Human effort depends on grace even as it invites it. Whatever degree of divine union we may reach bears no proportion to our effort. It is the sheer gift of divine love.

41. Jesus did not teach a specific method of meditation or bodily discipline for quieting the imagination, memory and emotions. We should choose a spiritual practice adapted to our particular and natural disposition. We

must also be willing to dispense with it when called by the Spirit to surrender to his direct guidance. The Spirit is above every method or practice. To follow his inspiration is the sure path to perfect freedom.

42. What Jesus proposed to his disciples as the Way is his own example: the forgiveness of everything and everyone and the service of others in their needs. His final teaching: "Love one another as I have loved you."

Look for more previously-unpublished
offerings from Father Thomas Keating
forthcoming from Homebound Publications.

God Is All In All (2023)

That We May Be One (2023)

God Is Love (2024)

The Gift Of Life (2024)

Heartfulness (2025)

ABOUT THE AUTHOR

Beloved Trappist monk Thomas Keating is best known as one of the primary founders of the Centering Prayer movement, which made the contemplative dimension of Christianity accessible through a simple method of silent, still meditation. He is also known as the convener of the Snowmass Interreligious Conference, which helped spawn the global Inter-spiritual movement. Keating's open invitation to people of all walks to embark on a spiritual journey, coupled with his emphasis on the oneness of all creation, made him a 20th-century harbinger of 21st-century ideals.

HOMEBOUND
PUBLICATIONS

WAYFARER

BASED IN THE BERKSHIRE MOUNTAINS, MASS.

The Wayfarer Magazine. Since 2012, *The Wayfarer* has been offering literature, interviews, and art with the intention to inspires our readers, enrich their lives, and highlight the power for agency and change-making that each individual holds. By our definition, a wayfarer is one whose inner-compass is ever-oriented to truth, wisdom, healing, and beauty in their own wandering. *The Wayfarer's* mission as a publication is to foster a community of contemplative voices and provide readers with resources and perspectives that support them in their own journey.

Wayfarer Books is our newest imprint! After nearly 10 years in print, *The Wayfarer Magazine* is branching out from our magazine to become a full-fledged publishing house offering full-length works of eco-literature!

Wayfarer Farm & Retreat is our latest endeavor, springing up in the Berkshire Mountains of Massachusetts. Set to open to the public in 2024, the 15 acre retreat will offer workshops, farm-to-table dinners, off-grid retreat cabins, and artist residencies.

WWW.WAYFARERBOOKS.ORG

CPSIA information can be obtained
at www.ICGtesting.com
Printed in the USA
JSHW051912170223
37912JS00003B/3

9 781953 340542